Old DENNISTOUN

by

Andrew Stuart

QUARRY MASTERS.
BUILDING TRADES MERCHANTS.

TELEPHONE:
1125·1127.
BRIDGETON.

CONTRACTORS

GLASGOW

One of the Alexandra Transport Company's Sentinel waggons.

Foreword

In 1856 Mr Alexander Dennistoun directed the architect James Salmon (1805-88) to prepare plans of his properties for a new suburb called Dennistoun. The first buildings, villas, were erected in Wester Craigs and these were followed by terraces and four storey tenements. The boundary on the south side was part of Duke Street and the lands of Dunchattan and on the north the lands of Kennyhill, Townmill Road and the Molendinar Burn. The east side was marked by Cumbernauld Road, while the Necropolis and the Molendinar Burn marked the west.

During the development of this area the names of the country mansions and estates were retained. These were Golfhill, Whitehill, Craig Park, Broompark, Meadow Park, Haghill, and Wester and Easter Craigs.

In 1864, Mr Dennistoun extended these boundaries by acquiring the properties of Annfield and Bellfield from the representatives of Mr John Reid, who had intended feuing out these lands but unfortunately he died before he could do this.

The Last Car for Dennistoun

© Copyright 1995 Andrew Stuart
First published in the United Kingdom, 1995, Reprinted 2001
By Stenlake Publishing, 54-58 Mill Square, Catrine, Ayrshire. KA5 6RD
Telephone/Fax: 01290 551122
e-mail: sales@stenlake.co.uk website: www.stenlake.co.uk
ISBN 1-872074-67-7

The church in this view was called the Primitive Methodist Church of Alexandra Parade and the building is now the lodgeroom and social club of Lodge St Andrew No. 465.

Directly across the road was Stephen Mitchell's "Prize Crop" tobacco factory. Built alongside in the late 1930s was the factory of John Player's, which produced Navy Cut cigarettes. During World War Two these factories were requisitioned by Rolls Royce who employed mainly women to manufacture parts for the Ministry of Aircraft Production.

After the war, Wills had a factory built next door which produced Capstan cigarettes. With the profusion of tobacco factories this part of Alexandra Parade gained the nickname "Tobacco Road".

Dennistoun Baths & Terrace. Glasgow.

Dennistoun Baths was a private swimming club from 1883 and their facilities were leased to the local secondary schools for swimming purposes. It is now the Masters Snooker Centre.

Behind and in front of this building were grasslands which were often used for sheep grazing and were known locally as the "Sheepy". Most of the land opposite was taken up by the massive Will's factory which is now vacant. Two places of worship are still located here. The Potters House Christian Centre which was once St Barnabas Episcopal Church was built in 1936 and Our Lady of Good Counsel Chapel which was designed by Gillespie, Kidd and Coia and built in 1966.

WHITEVALE BOWLING GREEN, GOLFHILL DRIVE, GLASGOW.

Whitevale Bowling Club is the second oldest private club in Glasgow and has been in existence since 1836. The club was originally situated in the Whitevale area before eventually settling at the top of Whitehill Street, where the grounds were, and still are, often used for championship competitions. The grounds are surrounded by villas and fine looking tenements, some of which are named and dated with Oak Knowe being built between 1898 and 1902. Another dates from 1875. Whitehill Street goes uphill from Duke Street to Golfhill Drive and then descends to Alexandra Parade where, at one time, five black granite pillars ensured that no through traffic was allowed.

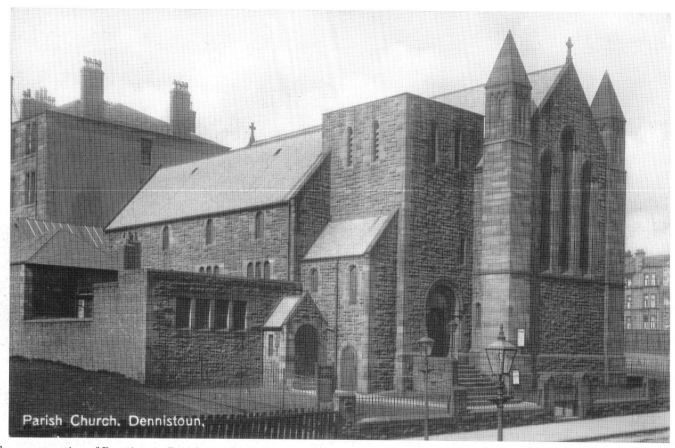

Parish Church. Dennistoun.

The congregation of Dennistoun Parish worshipped in temporary quarters until the church was built in 1907. It was situated on Armadale Street and cornered on to Golfhill Drive. An unusual feature of the church was that the choir and the organ were in the gallery behind the congregation and the minister.

Their football team was prominent in the Churches League and had its own ground between Armadale Street and Meadowpark Street. However, the pitch was taken over in 1935 by the Corporation of Glasgow and the site used for a new housing scheme in Ballindalloch Drive.

The congregation united with Dennistoun South and Blackfriars in May 1982 to become Dennistoun Blackfriars. The property was sold off, demolished and replaced by a modern brick tenement block.

Alexandra Parade Primary was one of several in Dennistoun. The others were Golfhill, Haghill, Bluevale, Dennistoun and Thomson Street. The architects were McWhannell and Rogerson and the school opened in 1897. Undoubtedly, they would be indignant with the later extensions erected in the playground.

Between Craigielea and Armadale Streets were once the courts of the Craigpark Tennis Club. They also had others at the side of two cinemas, the Parade and the Park. These courts were eventually utilised by Glasgow Corporation for post war housing.

From Craigielea Street onwards, that side of the Parade was regarded as a good shopping area. Many of the shopkeepers have gone - Black's the chemist, City Bakeries, Galbraith's, Massey's, Henderson's the newsagents and also that of Messer's, who displayed Dinky cars and Hornby train sets. Others were Warden's the butchers, Thomson's the fishmonger, Black's bakery and Melrose's dairy. The nearest Glasgow Eastern Co-op stores were in Roebank Street and others were in Cumbernauld Road. A post office was also there and there was another beyond Armadale Street which was near to 490 Alexandra Parade, once the address of the old Parade Cinema.

ALEXANDRA PARADE FROM MEADOWPARK ST. GLASGOW

After Meadowpark Street, the next one on the south side of the Parade was called Kaiser Street but was renamed Marne Street at the beginning of the First World War. This was also the name of the small picture house which later became known as the Park Cinema. Peculiarities of this house were that, once admitted, patrons had to queue inside for vacancies, the gallery was but three steps up from the back stalls, and the manager sprayed the auditorium at regular intervals with "Cromessol" perfumed essence, which was advertised on slides during the intermissions.

St Andrew's East United Free Church was formed in 1843 when the Reverend Doctor Nathaniel Paterson and 456 members of the congregation disrupted from St Andrew's Parish Church in Glasgow Cross. They first worshipped in the Black Bull Inn, Argyle Street, until their new church at the corner of Cathedral Street and North Hanover Street was ready in 1844. The architect was JT Rochead and these premises were sold in 1898. It is now part of McDonald's furniture showroom.

The UF Church depicted here was built in 1904 and the architect was James Miller. The halls were completed in 1899 to the designs of James Salmon II, the grandson of the man responsible for the planning of the district of Dennistoun, James Salmon.

The lands of Alexandra Park were laid out in 1866 and purchased by the City Improvement Trust from Walter Stewart of Haghill. They were extended when Easter Kennyhill was bought from the Dennistoun family. The Park was officially opened in 1870 by the Prince and Princess of Wales. In 1912, James Whitton, the Superintendent of Parks, reported his concern that obnoxious emissions from the nearby Blochairn Steelworks and the Provan Gasworks were damaging all but the hardiest of trees and shrubs. He needn't have worried for the steelworks have gone and the gasworks only store gas now instead of producing it from coal.

He would be proud of today's gardeners who have transformed those wide pavements into rosebeds and decked the entrance gates with brightly coloured flower baskets.

Alexandra Park, Glasgow.

The lawns at both sides of this wide promenade were once forbidden territory with cast iron signs indicating "Please Keep Off The Grass". This area was also patrolled by attendants, "parkies", who warned off trespassers by blowing hard on their whistles. Nowadays these grassy spaces are used by sunbathers, pic-nickers and playful children. Better use is made of the wide promenade as this now has central rosebeds and interspersed with bright annual flowers.

The shelter at the Sannox Gardens gate has long since been demolished and replaced by houses for the park gardeners.

This cast iron fountain is the centre piece of splendid floral displays and well cut lawns. The fountain was manufactured by Walter MacFarlane & Co. of Possilpark and was originally sited at Kelvingrove Park. It was a centre piece of the 1901 International Exhibition. Around 1910 it was transferred to Alexandra Park and was one of three which were cast by the MacFarlane's Saracen Foundry. The others can be found in the Town Hall Park, Warrington, and in the Zoological Grounds of Pretoria, South Africa. The designer was DW Stevenson and the figures represent Art, Literature, Science and Commerce.

Like most fountains in Glasgow, the waterworks are no longer in operation.

Bandstand, Alexandra Park.

A 1930s view of a typical audience at the then new bandstand. Concert parties and brass band concerts were held weekly from May to September throughout the Glasgow parks. They were advertised in local papers and also by the flying of the Union Jack from the park's flagpole on the day of the concert. Seats were charged for but just as many people saw the concerts for free by standing around the surrounding fences. Displays by local youth organisations and ceremonies such as the crowning of gala princesses took place during Saturday afternoons in the summer. Note, by the way, the alternative headgear to the "bunnet" - Anthony Eden hats, or as they are more properly called - Homburgs!

Children enjoyed cranking the paddle boats around the duck pond until they were whistled in by the park attendant whenever their tuppence worth had expired. These flat bottomed boats were extremely popular during the summer holidays and youngsters queued impatiently behind the pay box on the jetty. Their wait was occasionally relieved when the cry was heard, "Come in number so and so, your time is up."

Alas, today the pond is reserved strictly for the birds.

Strolling through the Park and Listen to the Band were not only song titles of Victorian days, but also part of their pleasures and pastimes. The musical programme for bands would mainly be of popular classics and operettas. Easy listening by today's standards!

Dennistoun's housing ended at the building in Aberfoyle Street, off Cumbernauld Road, and those open spaces beyond were later the Corporation of Glasgow's Haghill housing scheme of the early thirties. Perpetuated in this area are the names of former property owners - the family Todd, Walter Stewart of Haghill and John 'Iron' Gray of Carntyne.

PADDLING POOL, ALEX NDRA PARK, GLASGOW B 4329

This post war scene shows many changes from the one on the previous page. The bandstand has now become a paddling pool, known locally as the "sanny pond", with a rockery garden behind the seating. The small building on the right was the attendant's room and was also used as an old men's club which had an outdoor draughts board in front of it.

Beyond that there were three football pitches and dressing rooms. The pre-fab houses have long since been demolished and this area is now part of a jogging course. Of the two buildings at the top left, one was the Rex Picture House and the hanger-like one was a garage which has changed ownership many times.

Model yacht racing was a very popular hobby before the Second World War and many Glasgow parks had regattas in which clubs competed against each other. These slick vessels were either made by their owners or purchased from the Clyde Model Dockyard shop in the Argyll Arcade. At Alexandra Park, a shed was built to store these yachts.

Young children also sailed their smaller craft and clockwork motorboats. Another use of the pond by then was to fish for baggy minnies with a net and bamboo cane. Their catch was stored in jam jars or milk bottles with string handles attached to the tops.

In the 1970s, the pond was used by model boat enthusiasts who steered their craft by remote control.

Cumbernauld Road.

The shops and tenements depicted here were the last ones at this end of Dennistoun, and the last three streets were named Aberdour, Aberfeldy and Aberfoyle. Another street named Abernethy can be found off Duke Street. The railings in front of the tenement buildings were taken away in the Second World War scrap metal drives and were never replaced.

The tramcar routes which continued on to Riddrie and Millerston were the no.7 yellow car and the red no.8. Their journeys ended in the other direction at Bellahouston and Rouken Glen or Giffnock respectively.

ABERFELDY STREET.

Aberfeldy Street, like the adjacent Aberfoyle, was a steep street running downwards from Walter Street to Cumbernauld Road where shops were to be found. Unlike today, traffic was light and these thoroughfares could safely be used as playgrounds for the children.

Games such as Kick the Can, Leave-O, Hide an' Seek could be played by all. Girls also had peever and skipping ropes while boys raced around about with girds an' cleeks.

On frosty days, pavements were made into slippery slides until grown ups sprinkled these hazards with ashes. When the snow fell, out came the home made sledges.

Edinburgh Road opened in the early 1930s and its beginning, which can be seen on the right, continued as a boulevard through Carntyne out to Baillieston.

The building in the centre was the Rex Picture House which was demolished in 1974 and the area is now the site of a car show-room. The rooftop of another cinema can be seen on the extreme left. This opened in 1939 as the Riddrie and was later renamed the Vogue and is still in use today as a bingo hall. Both these cinemas duplicated their programmes with the Dennistoun and the Park respectively.

Aitken Street was officially the tramcar terminal for the Alexandra Park to Scoutstoun West route. This service was withdrawn on the last day of October 1959.

The tramcars shown here are "Coronation" type and were introduced in 1937. They were also known as "Exhibition" trams. Later there were modifications and these later trams were designated the "Coronation type Mark II" and one of these can be seen on page 21. These were sometimes known as "Cunarders" and the main visual difference was the style of destination board.

Haghill School is situated in Marwick Street between Aitken Street and Appin Road. It was built in 1904 in the contemporary style of Glasgow School Board buildings, consisting of three storey blocks in red sandstone.

In his book Pavements in the Sun, Jack House recalls his elementary days there. He tells of a special Lochgelly tawse supposedly in the possession of a tall gaunt teacher and one day Jack was held back by him for a misdemeanour. Expecting to be thrashed by the strap, he was most surprised when he was dismissed with a few sharp words but given no punishment. The teacher, who was a man of peace, later became an MP and was called Jimmy Maxton.

During the early years of the Second World War, Kennyhill School was an auxiliary fire station and was manned by these part time volunteers. Later, St Thomas's School in Riddrie became the main station. Other wartime stations were for two barrage balloon crews, one inside the back end of Alexandra Park and the other on Golfhill Cricket Club's ground in Meadowpark Street. On the northern side of Alexandra Parade and between Millburn and Milnpark Streets was an Air Raid Precaution Post which was stationed by wardens of the Civil Defence Corps.

St. Rollox Bowling Green, Dennistoun.

St Rollox Bowling Club was founded in 1857, taking the name of the Parliamentary Division of the district as their first green was in Glebe Street. Their second was at 137 Millburn Street from 1866-89 when they then shifted to an area in Wishart Street. At the end of 1902 they received a notice to quit from the Royal Infirmary which required the land for extensions to the hospital.

Fortunately, by 1904 Glasgow Corporation and the Parks Superintendent had agreed to lease ground at Alexandra Park where the club has since remained. The original club house, shown here, has been greatly extended and now covers the width of the green and is very popular for social gatherings.

This is the end of Alexandra Parade as the street becomes Cumbernauld Road at this junction. It was one of the many busy spots at peak times. The congestion has now been lessened hereabouts, mainly because of the M8 Motorway and the redesigning of the junction to ease the flow of traffic.

To the left is Appin Road, and not far along was the ground of Dennistoun Waverley FC who played under the auspices of the Scottish Junior Football Association in the Central League. They were a breakaway group from Bridgeton Waverley and were formed shortly after the war. Both clubs are now defunct.

Another view of the junction which shows the red sandstone tenements of Kennyhill Square, built in 1908, and in between are the greens of St Rollox Bowling Club. It was around this square that Glasgow's most popular author and reporter, Jack House, spent his childhood days.

The empty premises of Andrew Cochrane, provision merchant, caused controversy in the 1960s when the new owners applied for a spirit licence and later opened up as the "Lea Rig" public house.

In bygone days every tramcar had an honesty box where passengers could put their fare if the conductor was too busy and unable to collect. This can be readily seen on the left hand side of the platform.

This tramcar is about to go over the railway bridge which had a weight restriction of ten tons. After crossing the bridge it would pass Bannatyne Avenue as it rounded the bend at Alexandra Park Street. There were quite a few shops here including a barber's, a cafe, billiard halls and small workshops for electricians, joiners and plumbers. All of these premises were demolished and the street widened. It is now a major route leading to the M8 Motorway and to Blochairn Fruit Market.

To the extreme right is a billboard advertising the films for the Scotia Cinema which was in nearby Millerston Street. It survived for a time as a popular bingo hall but the cry "House" can no longer be heard.

Across the street and over the wall was Duke Street Station and the railway line. On the other side of this was Paton Street in which was the Dennistoun Tramway Depot. There were also two other factories; John Wallace and Sons, an engineering firm which manufactured agricultural implements and also Beatties Bakeries, famed for their bread, cakes and a diamond shaped biscuit, half covered in chocolate and called an Ayton Sandwich.

Seen on the left is a scooter, another mode of transport common in the 1950s and 1960s. Makes such as Lambretta, Vespa, Heinkel and BSA Sunbeam were very popular with the younger set.

Duke Street is reputed to be named after the Duke of Montrose, whose lodging looked over it, and the street is claimed to be the longest in Great Britain beating London's Oxford Street by several yards.

Facing this junction, Miller Street East (now Millerston Street) can be seen. Many of the street names came from the surnames of the spouses of the Dennistoun family (Finlay, Onslow, Ingleby, Oakley and Wood) or their residences (Armadale, Garthland and Roselea). Others were from property owners such as John Reid (Reidvale Street), James Sword (Sword Street) and Thomson Street, named after the proprietor of the Annfield Pottery.

Annfield and Bellfield were once villas, named after Ann and Isobel, the wives of James Tennent and John McAlpine respectively.

Meadowpark Street was en route for the no. 6/6A Corporation bus in the heyday of the tramcar era. Situated in this street were two schools, Dennistoun Public (now St Denis Primary) and the demolished Onslow Drive Junior Secondary. Two churches still exist. These are Dennistoun Evangelical Union (now the Christian Friendship and Education Centre) and Dennistoun Baptist. There were also the grounds and pavilion of the Golfhill Cricket Club, which are now part of Whitehill Polytechnic School and its playing fields. At the Alexandra Parade end was the New Parade Cinema (now lounge bars and a restaurant), while at the Duke Street end there was a public house, a rarity within the boundaries of Old Dennistoun.

This church in Armadale Street was first known as Dennistoun United Free and the architects were James Salmon and William, his son. The church later became Rutherford United and was renamed Dennistoun Central in 1975 when the congregations of Rutherford, Whitevale, Bluevale and Trinity Duke Street were united. The church organ came from Trinity Duke Street and was manufactured by the renowned firm of Father Willis.

It is worthwhile recalling that before this church was erected in 1874, temporary accommodation consisted of a ramshackle wooden hut in Whitehill Gardens. As a consequence of this, worshippers would move from one side to the other to dodge the rain-drops and would often put up their umbrellas during the sermon.

From Cumbernauld Road to Bellgrove, Duke Street had shops a-plenty for housewives looking out for household bargains and keen prices for groceries. Many of these shops are now displaying "To Let" signs instead of goods, as the nearby supermarkets and the "Forge" shopping complex have taken away their trade.

The tramcars have gone, but the no. 46 bus still journeys on having extended its route to Robroyston instead of Queenslie, but still running to Castlemilk. When asked by a stranger if the Castlemilk service was a good one, one local replied that it should be, it serves Pat Lally country.

One of the first buildings in Whitehill Street was Dennistoun United Presbyterian Church. A petition was presented to that Presbytery to form a new congregation in the north east of the city and this was granted in June 1869. The church was built the following year and was later renamed Whitehill United Presbyterian. On 6th May 1982, a union with Blackfriars, Dennistoun Parish and Dennistoun South saw the church renamed Dennistoun Blackfriars.

Sir Andrew Pettigrew of Pettigrew and Stephen's Department Store in Sauchiehall Street lived nearby when he was a youth. Another well known business in the street was Dales of Dennistoun, a cycling shop.

Whitehill Senior Secondary School was built in the 1890s by the Glasgow Education Department and had a most successful academic record. Among its former pupils were Jack House, Jack Short (Pa Logan), Alistair Gray, Adam McNaughton, Ricki Fulton and Dorothy Paul.

In 1939 the Education Department decided that Whitehill should amalgamate with the nearby Onslow Drive Junior Secondary. There were protests and demonstrations against such a move but the declaration of war diminished this issue. Both schools have now been demolished and a new one "Whitehill Polytechnic" is erected partly on the site of the old Onslow Drive School.

GLASGOW EAST-END INDUSTRIAL EXHIBITION.

The East End Industrial Exhibition opened on 23rd December 1890 inside the buildings of the Old Reformatory for Boys which was built in 1836 at 327 Duke Street. A season ticket cost seven shillings and sixpence and admission was a shilling till 1st January 1891 when it was reduced to sixpence. The next day had the largest attendance of 21,608 with the total figure being 747,873 by 21st April when the exhibition closed. £3000 was raised for the building fund of the People's Palace.

The main attractions were the 3000 capacity concert hall, which was well filled each evening, Wilmot's Canadian Switchback, Edison's latest phonograph and the Art and Photograph Galleries. From November 1891 until February 1892, Colonel William F Cody, better known as Buffalo Bill, staged his "Wild West" show here. He returned to Glasgow again in 1904, to the delight of many.

This East End Industrial Exhibition opened on 8th December 1903, when 5000 guests attended the opening ceremony. A total of 12,654 visited on the first day and the top daily attendance was on the first Monday when 26,217 entered through the turnstiles. Admission was sixpence, season tickets were seven shillings and sixpence each, and a book of thirty admission tickets could be had for ten shillings.

The Glasgow Royal Infirmary was to benefit from the proceeds for their reconstruction plans. The medals, which were awarded to successful exhibitors, showed the City's Coat of Arms on the obverse side. The reverse had "Industry", the Royal Infirmary and the Cathedral with the inscription 'For the Glasgow Royal Infirmary'. The attendance was a remarkable 908,897 by 9th April 1904, but the net profit was a mere £212.

The new Dennistoun Palais de Danse opened in 1938 after a fire of 1936 had gutted the old Palais which had opened in 1922 upon the site of a skating rink. The new hall's capacity was for 1800 dancers and the air conditioning plant was often over taxed on popular nights. The dance floor was the biggest in Glasgow and it was calculated that ten circuits around the hall measured a mile.

For many a year, the resident musicians were Lauri Blandford and his Orchestra, an eleven piece outfit with Maisie McLellan as their singer. Lauri led from the piano except when he played accordion for tangos.

After 1962, other forms of entertainment were tried but failed to attract the crowds and the "Denny Pally" was then taken over by the "Fine Fare" supermarket chain. *(Picture reproduced courtesy of Strathclyde Regional Archives).*

The tramcar has just passed Hillfoot Street which has seen throngs of people pass up it on their way to various East End Exhibitions, Wild West Shows and other such events held in the Old Reformatory until it was knocked down. On part of these grounds, Whitevale School had a wooden annexe built and also had a makeshift rugby pitch. At one time there was also a roller skating rink and later dancing daft folk flocked to the "Pally", old and new, from the 1920s to the 1960s. After this, housewives hoped to make their day by having a winning night out at the Bingo. The street is not so busy now as even the GPO sorting office has gone, to be replaced by a paint, paper and paste warehouse.

On 15th May 1901, Mr Andrew Carnegie sent a letter to the Lord Provost gifting the sum of £100,000 to provide fourteen district libraries for Glasgow. The architect, James R Rhind, must have had a busy time in those early Edwardian days because in 1905-6, seven of these were erected to his plans. They were Woodside, Maryhill, Dennistoun, Bridgeton, Parkhead, Govanhill and Hutchesontown, all of which were built in classical style, adorned with sculptured panels and figures. Four of them have similar domes with a statue representing Literature at the top. Dennistoun Library opened on 29th December 1905 with a total stock of 9874 books in its lending department.

Regent Place U. F. Church, Dennistoun.

The congregation of Regent Place Church was formed in 1817 when they broke away from the Duke Street Anti-Burgher Church. The properties of both churches were taken over by the North British Railway in 1877 for the formation of the College Goods Station and yards. The new Regent Place Church was located in Craigpark, Dennistoun while that of Duke Street was built in Cathedral Square. This is now Glasgow Evangelical Church. In 1941, the union of Regent Place and Cathedral Square took place and the members worshipped in the Dennistoun Church until the congregation dissolved in 1960. The premises were sold to the Education Authority and were utilised by the nearby Whitehill School. The church was eventually destroyed by a fire in 1983.

It has been rightly said that Annfield Place is on the wrong side as the villa and property were on the south side of Duke Street. These terraced houses were first occupied by ministers and doctors and are now used mainly by lawyers and insurance companies as offices.

The church spire is that of Blackfriars, which came to Westercraigs in 1877 when the NBR acquired their church in the College Lands. Their first minister here was Reverend Thomas Sommerville who was a leading light in establishing the East End Exhibition as well as being the author of several books, one of which was "George Square" (published in 1890). This gives descriptive sketches of the buildings therein.

On official maps of Glasgow the cross-roads of Duke Street with Westercraigs and Bellgrove Street is called "Kings Cross", but to locals this has always been simply "Bellgrove". The tenements on the left hand side have been torn down and replaced by the approaches to the city abattoir. All the other buildings are intact, although Blackfriars Church and manse have been converted into luxury flats.

Westercraigs, incidentally, was the first street in Dennistoun, followed by Craigpark, Broompark Drive and the terraces of Seton, Clayton and Oakley. Sir William Arrol once lived at the corner of Oakley Terrace and Craigpark.

Bellgrove Street was once known as Witches Lone and is said to have been first used by the masons who built the Cathedral and who lived in Rutherglen. Drovers used this road for cattle to cross the Clyde at Dalmarnock ford.

On the western side, Bellgrove housed the cattle market. The site of this is now used as a car auction market. There is a massive reconstruction programme in progress with many parts of the facade of the old market being retained. There is also a railway station where the lines branch out northwards to Springburn and east to Airdrie.

At the southwest corner of Bellgrove and Reidvale Street stood the Bellgrove United Presbyterian Church which began as a mission under the responsibility of the Greyfriars Church in Albion Street, and eventually came to Dennistoun in 1870.

In November 1972 the congregation joined with Whitehill to become Dennistoun South. The Bellgrove building was then demolished, as it was considered to be unsafe, sited as it was at the top of the railway embankment.

Bellgrove Church's football team had their own enclosed ground in Roselea Drive near to Cumbernauld Road. During the summer, well attended matches were played amongst the local church football teams. The football pitch, which is in the sports ground of Whitehill Polytechnic, was once that of Bellgrove.

This city bound tramcar has just passed the Eastern District Hospital, erected at the beginning of this century. Demolished in 1994, except for its red sandstone reception block, the hospital was often referred to merely as "Duke Street".

The adjoining tenements and those stretching to Ark Lane were knocked down by the early 1970s. They were replaced by new housing and play areas with the old names of Dunchattan, McIntosh and Fisher being retained.

George MacIntosh set up his dyeworks and mansion on these lands in 1777. He called the mansion Dunchattan. His son, Charles, invented the waterproof material known by their surname. Fisher Street, by the way, was named after Charles MacIntosh's wife whose maiden name was Fisher.

In the foreground in this aerial view are St Anne's Chapel, Presbytery and gardens which was built in 1931 in Whitevale Street. Beyond that is the steeple of Dennistoun Central and to the far left is that of Dennistoun Blackfriars in Whitehill Street. The school can also be located and the white patch in front of it is the roof of the Dennistoun Palais, now a Solo supermarket. Another rooftop is the triangular shape at the top left which is that of Our Lady of Good Counsel Chapel in Craigpark. The tobacco factories are in front of this and at the extreme left corner are the extensions to the Royal Infirmary.

This 1970 aerial view shows some of the district's industrial history with the long established firm of Thomas Hinshelwood & Company (1878), manufacturers of paints, varnishes and oils, in the foreground. Beyond that is the Netherfield Chemical Works or R&J Garroway (1817), makers of sulphuric acid and fertilisers. William Reid & Sons, Wireworkers, another long standing firm, was located nearby. The Glasgow Corporation Cleansing Yard and incinerator in Haghill Road had already been demolished, as had the tenements of Netherfield and the bottom part of Todd Street. Bluevale School in Abernethy Street can be seen in the midst of the scheme, but later met with the same fate as many of the buildings in this area.

The railway was electrified in the early 1960s and was used at that time by the "Blue Trains"

Hereabouts, Duke Street meets Carntyne Road and the resulting junction was known as Netherfield Cross. The four storey tenements of Netherfield and Plant Streets adjoined on to the chemical works right round Duke Street to Craigmore Street. All of these have been knocked down and this area is now grassland.

This photograph was taken in November 1955 and at the time Glasgow still had three evening newspapers. They were the "Times, Citizen an' the News". The News, advertised on the side of the tram, was only to last another year before ceasing publication in 1956.

Although Beatties Bread vans were still trundling in and out of the nearby bakery, they have also vanished. Now, deliveries are by British Bakeries from the enlarged bakery and garage complex now situated in Duke Street.

"Green Cars go East" was the apt title of a play about Glasgow life by the playwright, Paul Vincent Carroll. This was the regular colour serving such routes as Baillieston, Airdrie and Dalmarnock. Occasionally these journeys were shortened at the Dennistoun terminus, just beyond the beginning of Carntyne Road. At one time this was the terminus of the Kelvinside - Dennistoun run.

These high entranced tenements have long since been reduced to rubble and "doo-cots" are now scattered about the open spaces.

Nearby is the defunct Carntyne Greyhound Stadium, one of four major ones once to be found in the city. The others were White City, Albion and the only survivor, Shawfield.

The most popular tram terminus for many Dennistounians was that of Millerston, where they could disembark for a boat trip around Hogganfield Loch during weekends or on long summer evenings. In addition to this, rowing boats could be hired for the half hour. The island in the centre of the loch is a bird sanctuary where several species of duck can be seen.

Visitors also had the choice of a pleasant stroll around the pathways, a game of pitch an' putt or a refreshment in the tea room where a magnificent view of the loch and surroundings could be seen. There was also a good picnic area used by organisations and Sunday Schools for their annual outings.

Blackhill Locks, Riddrie

An interesting walk for local youngsters was along the canal bank. At the Millburn Bridge, players of Townhead Quoits Club could be observed tossing heavy discs onto soft clay squares. Passing Blochairn Works, onlookers were fascinated by the magnetic grab lifting scrap metal and discharging it. The biggest thrill was standing at the derelict Blackhill Locks which were then like water-falls. Further along were the grim walls of Barlinnie, the "Sugarolly Mountains" (yellow, white and black chemical deposits) plus Craigend sports grounds belonging to Whitehill Secondary School. The outward journey ended at Milncroft Bridge, then on to the country track of Stepps Road and homewards via Edinburgh Road to the delights of Dennistoun.